When Your Pet Dies

A Healing Handbook for Kids

Written by
Victoria Ryan

Illustrated by
R. W. Alley

D1511383

ONE
CARING
PLACE

Abbey Press
St. Meinrad, IN 47577

To
Alex, Zachary, Michael, Shaun, Chris, Kevin
in memory of our dog
Amber

Text © 2003 Victoria Ryan
Illustrations © 2003 St. Meinrad Archabbey
Published by One Caring Place
Abbey Press
St. Meinrad, Indiana 47577

Library of Congress Catalog Number
2003096172

ISBN 978-0-87029-376-4

Printed in the United States of America

A Message to Parents, Teachers, and Other Caring Adults

Losing a pet is often a child's first experience with death. Whether the pet was given away, ran away, or died of natural causes—the sadness following its loss is true grief.

Your child's pet was the epitome of loyalty and unconditional love, and the more your child interacted with it, the sadder he'll be. The death of a goldfish, for example, may seem trivial—but for a child who confided secrets to the fish, who sat near the bowl whenever he was lonely or afraid, the loss is quite significant. His grief is intensified if the pet was a gift from an absent parent or close relative, or if it performed a service such as a seeing-eye or guard dog.

Ask your child if she wants to see or hold her pet. Ask if she wants a funeral. Don't hide your own emotions. This is a sad time; let your child see that grief is a normal response to loss. Don't rush to replace the pet; rather, honor the unique place this animal held in your lives.

A very young child will grieve in spurts. An older child will ask questions: Where did my pet go? Is my pet in pain? Will Mom or Dad die too? Listen carefully to your child's questions and let your beliefs guide your answers.

Encourage your child to express her feelings: Make a pet scrapbook and write captions for the pictures. Create a memory box and include the pet's leash, tag, or bowl. Ask if your child would like to give the remaining items to an animal shelter, or donate some of her allowance for pet research.

Just as a pet teaches a child to value life, the loss of a pet can teach a child empathy for the pain of others. A child who does not receive support when her pet dies, however, may learn to harden her emotions to pets and people.

Your child will never forget his or her pet, or the day it died. By handling this loss with sensitivity and gentleness, these memories can be a source of loving comfort for you and your child.

—Victoria Ryan

Losing a Pet

Your pet might be very old or very sick. Maybe she was hit by a car, or ran out of the yard and hasn't come home for a long time.

Perhaps your pet has to be given away because your family is moving, or because your sister is allergic to her. Maybe she has to be taken away because she hurt someone.

Your parent might say, "Your pet needs to go away" or "Your pet is going to die." You feel very, very sad.

What "Dying" Means

"Dying" means your pet's body stops working and cannot be fixed. Dying means you will not be able to play with her again. All pets die—birds and bunnies, fish and ferrets, cats, dogs, and horses.

When it's time for your pet to die, she will act differently. Your dog may move very slowly. Your rabbit's eyes may seem tired and droopy. Your cat may not walk across your sofa or chase the toy mouse. You might tap on your aquarium, but your fish may not swim to you.

You want to make your pet better, but you can't. It is a sad day.

Saying Good-bye

Your parent might say, "Your pet needs to go to the vet for the last time." That means your pet will be dead soon. You need to say good-bye to her.

Hug your pet and tell her you love her. Tell her she was the best pet in the whole world. Ask your parent to take a picture of you with your pet.

You might write a good-bye letter to your pet and tie it to a balloon. When your pet dies, let the balloon float up to heaven with her.

When Your Pet Dies Suddenly

Sometimes pets die without anyone knowing. You might walk into your room and find your gerbil lying quietly in his cage. You might tickle your cat, but she won't move. You might call your lizard's name, but he won't look at you. You might touch your bird, but it feels stiff and cold.

You can still say good-bye to your pet. You could wrap your pet's small body in one of your shirts and hug him one last time. You could cover him with his favorite blanket, and hold his paw like you always did.

Tell your pet you will miss him very much and will never forget him. He will hear what you say from heaven.

Pet Heaven

Heaven is a beautiful place where God takes care of pets and people after they die. Your pet will not have pain in heaven. He will always be happy there.

Ask your parents what they think your pet is doing in heaven. Could your rabbit be hopping from one cloud to the next? Could angels be riding your horse, or playing catch with your dog?

You can't visit heaven, and your pet can't visit you. But he can hear you when you pray. Tell your pet how you feel.

It's Okay to Cry

Although your pet is safe and happy, you are still sad. You miss your pet. You keep loving it, even though it is gone.

You might wonder if it is okay to cry about your pet. It is. Your pet loved you and made you feel special. He was your friend. It's natural to cry.

Your parents might cry. Your sister and brother may cry. It's okay for everybody to cry, no matter how old they are.

Some people don't cry even when they are sad. It's okay not to cry, too.

Tell People About Your Pet

People who knew your pet may want to say good-bye, too. You might make "announcement cards." An announcement card tells the name of your pet and the day it died. You can draw a picture of your pet on the card or put his photograph inside. You can write a letter or a poem about him.

Give the cards to your neighbors and friends. Mail them to your grandparents, aunts, and uncles. Show them to your teachers and classmates.

Your Pet's Funeral

A funeral is a ceremony that honors a pet that has died. People gather and say nice things about your pet. They will say they are sorry he died. They will tell funny stories about him. Hearing how much people enjoyed your pet will help you feel better.

Do you think people will remember how fast your cat could chase a squirrel? Will they remember when your dog jumped in the school bus and made the driver and children laugh?

What Happens to Your Pet

If your pet is small, your family may bury her in your backyard. If your pet is large, they may use a "pet cemetery."

A pet cemetery is a beautiful big yard where many pets are buried. The spot where your pet is buried is called a "grave." You can put a stone on your pet's grave so you will always know where she is. You can carve her name on it. Maybe you can plant flowers or a tree there.

Some pets, like horses, are too big to bury in your backyard. Veterinarians help people with big animals to know what to do.

Scary Feelings

You might have strange feelings you never had before. You may cry even when you try not to. You may have a hard time sleeping, or have trouble listening in school. You might not feel hungry, or want to play.

You may dream that your pet is still with you, sitting on your bed or climbing in its cage. You may be afraid that you or someone in your family will die or go away, just like your pet.

Most people live much longer than pets. And you will always have someone to love you and take care of you.

It's Nobody's Fault

You may feel angry. You may be mad at the car that hit your pet. You may be mad at the veterinarian and your parents for not saving her life. You may be mad at yourself for leaving the gate open the day she ran away. You may even be mad at her for running away or for dying.

It's no one's fault that your pet is gone. And no matter how mad you feel, no one can bring your pet back again. Even being very, very good will not bring her back.

You took good care of your pet. You fed her and gave her toys. You washed her and brushed her even when you didn't feel like it. Your pet was lucky to have you.

Talking Helps

Talking to your parents or another grownup will help your sad feelings go away. If you don't know what to say, they will help you find the words. You might talk about the day you got your pet. You might talk about the ways your pet was special.

Look at pictures to help you remember the happy times you had with your pet. Did you put bows and reindeer antlers on your cat at Christmas? Did you lean against your dog when you watched television on the floor? Did your gerbil get loose in the house and scare your Mom's friends? Did your rabbit eat the brownies your Dad made for the school bake sale?

How Long Will You Be Sad?

Your pet was a member of your family. She ate with you, slept with you, maybe even went on vacation with you.

She played with you anytime you wanted. She did tricks whenever you told her to. She ran around her cage or licked you every time you came home. She stayed by you when you were sick.

Your pet never got mad at you. She always loved you, even if you were in trouble. You told your pet secrets you could not tell anyone else.

You will always love your pet, but you will not always feel this sad. Your sadness will go away a little each day, if you do what your pet taught you...